Counting Books

10 9 8 Polar Animals!

A Counting Backward Book

by Rebecca Fjelland Davis

Reading Consultant: Gail Saunders-Smith, PhD

Capstone press

Mankato, MN

A+ Books are published by Capstone Press,
151 Good Counsel Drive, P.O. Box 669, Mankato, Minnesota 56002.
www.capstonepress.com

1 2 3 4 5 6 11 10 09 08 07 06

Library of Congress Cataloging-in-Publication Data
Davis, Rebecca Fjelland.
10, 9, 8 Polar Animals!: A Counting Backward Book / by Rebecca Fjelland Davis.
p. cm.—(A+ books. Counting books)
Summary: "Simple text and photographs introduce polar animals and count backward from
ten"—Provided by publisher.
Includes bibliographical references and index.
ISBN-13: 978-0-7368-6374-2 (hardcover)
ISBN-10: 0-7368-6374-5 (hardcover)
1. Counting—Juvenile literature. 2. Animals—Polar regions—Juvenile literature. I. Title: Ten,
nine, eight. II. Title. III. Series.
QA113.D376 2007
513.2'11—dc22   2005034932

Credits
Jenny Marks, editor; Ted Williams, designer; Kelly Garvin, photo researcher/photo editor

Photo Credits
Bruce Coleman Inc./Gordon Langsbury, 6 (bottom right); John Shaw, 7 (top left);
    Tom Brakefield, 22–23
Corbis/Paul A. Souders, 13 (bottom right); Theo Allofs, 18
Digital Vision, front cover, 3, 26 (polar bears), 27 (penguins), 28
Lynn M. Stone, 20–21
Minden Pictures/Flip de Nooyer/Foto Natura, 14; Jim Brandenburg, 8–9;
    Michio Hoshino, 4–5; Rinie Van Muers/Foto Natura, 16–17; Yva Momatiuk/John
    Eastcott, 12 (top right, bottom right)
Peter Arnold/Fritz Polking, 10; Klein, 24–25; Steven Kazlowski, 13 (top left)
Robert McCaw, 6 (top right, bottom right, top left, middle); 7 (bottom left, top right,
    bottom right)
Shutterstock/Halldor Eiriksson, 27 (terns), 29; Koval, back cover, (musk ox);
    Kris Mercer, 26 (puffin); Matthias Deck, 12 (top left), 13 (top right)

Note to Parents, Teachers, and Librarians
10, 9, 8 Polar Animals!: A Counting Backward Book uses color photographs and a
nonfiction format to introduce children to various types of polar animals while building
mastery of basic counting skills. It is designed to be read aloud to a pre-reader or to
be read independently by an early reader. The images help early readers and listeners
understand the text and concepts discussed. The book encourages further learning by
including the following sections: How Many, Facts about Polar Animals, Glossary, Read
More, Internet Sites, and Index. Early readers may need assistance using these features.

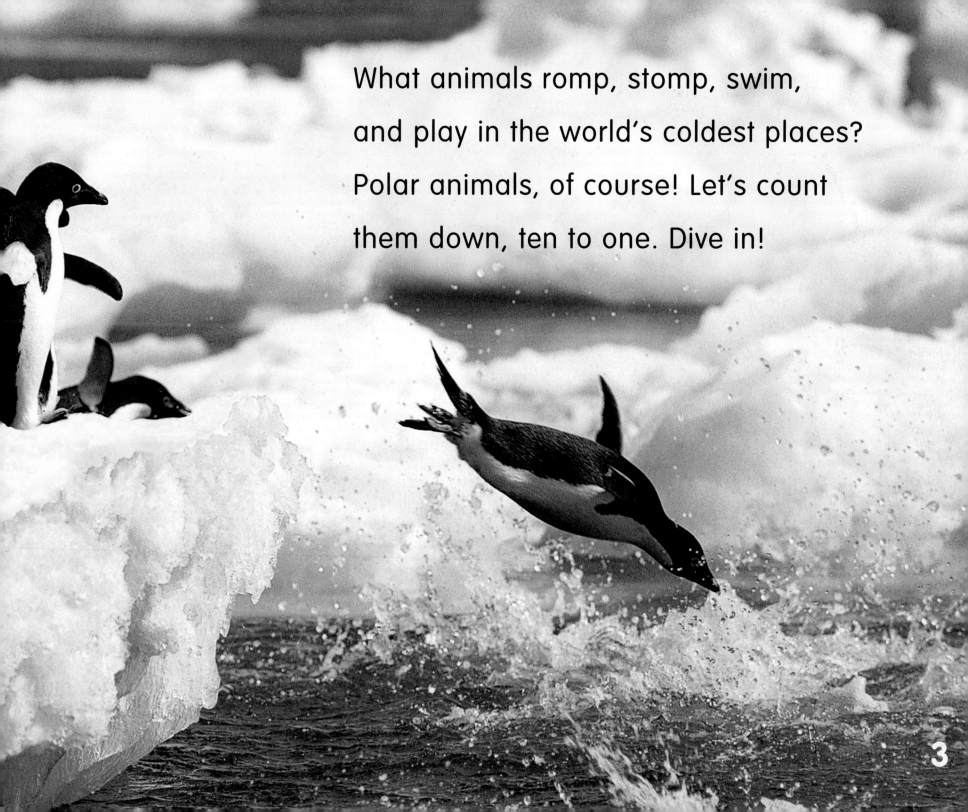

What animals romp, stomp, swim, and play in the world's coldest places? Polar animals, of course! Let's count them down, ten to one. Dive in!

10

Ten strong musk oxen make a wall
of horns and fur. Even in the wind,
this herd stays safe and warm.

Nine arctic terns swoop and dive into the water. In a flash, they catch a meal of tasty fish.

9

Eight arctic hares look like little lumps of snow. Pure white fur hides these hares from hungry wolves.

10
9
8
7
6
5
4
3
2
1

Six chubby penguins waddle across the ice. Where is number seven?

6

Six big caribou travel together to look for food. Each winter, caribou shed their antlers. In spring, they grow a pointy new pair.

10
9
8
7
6
5
4
3
2
1

13

Five little puffins have big, webbed feet for swimming. They come to shore in spring to build nests along the cliffs.

4

Four flabby walruses nap on the ice. They aren't lazy, they are just warming up in the sun!

10 9 8 7 6 5 4 3 2 1

3

Three fuzzy polar bears snuggle in the snow. Cubs live with their mother until they are almost three years old.

Two tundra wolves bound down an icy path. Wide, furry paws help wolves race through the snow.

10
9
8
7
6
5
4
3
2
1

22

One baby harp seal takes
a snooze in the snow.

23

Puffins, musk oxen, penguins, and arctic terns. Only the coolest animals live in polar places! Which polar animal is your favorite?

How Many?

Polar bears

Puffins

Arctic terns

Penguins

Facts about Polar Animals

Puffins only leave the water to build nests and raise their chicks. Expert fishers, puffins can carry more than 40 little fish in their big, curved bills.

Penguins look funny when they waddle, but they are excellent swimmers. Emperor penguins can dive down 700 feet (213 meters) and can stay underwater for more than 15 minutes at a time.

Polar bears have black noses and toes. They also have black skin beneath their white fur. The dark skin holds heat and keeps the polar bears warm.

Musk oxen live in groups of 10 to 20. When they sense danger, musk oxen protect their young by forming a circle around them. They snort loudly when anything bothers them.

Both male and female walruses have big tusks and bristly mustaches. Walruses hook their tusks on the ice to help pull themselves out of the water.

Arctic terns fly from the North Pole to the South Pole and back again every year. Arctic terns make the longest migration of any bird in the world.

Glossary

antler (ANT-lur)—a large, branching, bony growth on the head; caribou have antlers.

arctic (ARK-tik)—extremely cold and wintry

cub (KUHB)—a young polar bear

hare (HAIR)—an animal that looks like a large rabbit with long, strong back legs

herd (HURD)—a large group of animals

migrate (MYE-grate)—to move from one area to another as the seasons change

tusk (TUHSK)—a long, pointed tooth

waddle (WAHD-uhl)—to take short steps while moving from side to side

Read More

Glassman, Jackie. *Amazing Arctic Animals.*
All Aboard Science Reader. New York: Grosset
& Dunlap, 2002.

Macken, JoAnn Early. *Polar Animals.* Animal
Worlds. Milwaukee: Gareth Stevens, 2002.

Tatham, Betty. *Penguin Chick.*
Let's-Read-and-Find-Out-Science.
New York: HarperCollins, 2002.

Vogel, Julia. *Polar Animals: Explore the
Fascinating Worlds of—.* Minnetonka, Minn.:
NorthWord Press, 2002.

Internet Sites

FactHound offers a safe, fun way to find Internet sites related to
this book. All of the sites on FactHound have been researched by
our staff.

Here's how:

1. Visit *www.facthound.com*

2. Choose your grade level.

3. Type in this book ID **0736863745** for age-appropriate sites.
   You may also browse subjects by clicking on letters, or by
   clicking on pictures and words.

4. Click on the **Fetch It** button.

FactHound will fetch the best sites for you!

Index